IF EXTINCT BEASTS C

# PREHIS

# SEA BEASTS

Thanks to the creative team:
Senior Editor: Alice Peebles
Consultant: Neil Clark
Fact Checker: Kate Mitchell
Design: www.collaborate.agency



Hungry Tomato™
A division of Lerner Publishing Group, Inc.
241 First Avenue North
Minneapolis, MN 55401 USA

For reading levels and more information, look up this title at www.lernerbooks.com.

Main body text set in Franklin Gothic Book 11/12.
Typeface provided by International Typeface Corp.

**Library of Congress Cataloging-in-Publication Data**

The Cataloging-in-Publication Data for *Prehistoric Sea Beasts* is on file at the Library of Congress.
ISBN 978-1-5124-0634-4 (lib. bdg.)
ISBN 978-1-5124-1158-4 (pbk.)
ISBN 978-1-5124-0909-3 (EB pdf)

Manufactured in the United States of America
1-39307-21144-8/31/2016

**IF EXTINCT BEASTS CAME TO LIFE**

# PREHISTORIC SEA BEASTS

by Matthew Rake
Illustrated by Simon Mendez

WARNING!
These extinct beasts are not alive today, and the encounters seen in this book are not real. But just imagine if they were . . .

# CONTENTS

# THE BIG, THE BAD, AND THE UGLY

We all know that some very ugly, very scary dinosaurs ruled the Earth for over 100 million years. But they weren't the only creatures on the planet. Before—and after—the dinosaurs, there were other animals every bit as spine-chilling. Can you imagine what the world would be like if they came back to life? Well, you are about to find out . . .

***All life started in the sea***—and that's where the first big, scary animals appeared too. About 475 million years ago, there were massive sea scorpions with claws the size of tennis rackets and creatures in shells called nautiloids, the size of crocodiles.

Nautiloids

The first dinosaurs evolved 230 million years ago or even before, but they didn't rule the world right away. They couldn't—they were "only" 6–10 feet (2–3 meters) long, and some were ***just twice the size of chickens***. Even when dinosaurs had become ginormous, they had to watch out for crocodiles like *Sarcosuchus*. Four times as heavy as modern crocodiles, it liked a dinosaur for dinner.

Liopleurodon

In the seas, the top predators were reptiles such as the pliosaurs. A mighty one was the sleek and deadly 21-foot-long (6 m) *Liopleurodon* (*left*), here shown grabbing a plesiosaur called *Kimmerosaurus*. And the ***biggest pliosaur of all*** was *Pliosaurus funkei*.

Kimmerosaurus

***Mammals started evolving at the same time as dinosaurs.*** But they kept a low profile while the dinosaurs were around. For about 160 million years, most mammals were shrew-sized—any larger and they would have been gobbled up by hungry carnivorous dinosaurs.

After the dinosaurs died out, ***mammals grew to massive proportions.*** *Chalicotherium* (*left*) lived from about 28 million to 4 million years ago and stood about 9 feet (2.75 m) tall. Some mammals even evolved into sea creatures. Whales were once land mammals that started swimming in the seas to catch fish. On page 26 you can meet the biggest whale ever: *Livyatan*.

So prepare to plunge into the ancient oceans to discover not only giant sea scorpions and nautiloids but also truly epic marine monsters such as armor-plated *Dunkleosteus* (*below*). And if you think modern killer whales and great whites are dangerous . . . well, they are peace-loving pussycats compared to their awesome ancestors.

*Chalicotherium*

***If you've got the courage to witness the invasion of the prehistoric sea brutes, read on . . .*** just be prepared for some truly bizarre and scary encounters between modern creatures and these now-extinct beasts.

*Dunkleosteus*

# BIG NIPPER

## SEA SCORPION OR EURYPTERID

Let's face it, we are all a little frightened of scorpions—even though they are not very big. Can you imagine a scorpion bigger than an adult human? No? Well, meet the modern scorpion's bigger, badder prehistoric ancestors: the sea scorpions or eurypterids. They swam through ancient oceans and scuttled across sea floors, terrorizing every other living thing they came in contact with.

The sea scorpion chased down prey quickly with the help of its long tail and paddle-like swimming legs. Then it would go in for the kill with its huge claws. These were the size of tennis rackets and were covered with deadly spines, perfect for holding the unfortunate victim against the sea floor and then slicing and shredding it! The only thing it was missing was an underwater cutting board.

What if sea scorpions lived today? You'd have to feel sorry for the diver here. But if he's a strong swimmer, he'll probably lose no more than a flipper.

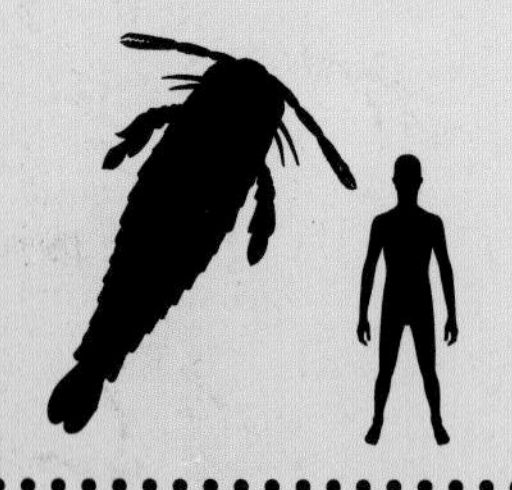

### EURYPTERID

**PRONOUNCED**
You-RIP-ter-id

**LIVED**
Seas worldwide, around 467 million–250 million years ago

**LENGTH**
Up to 8 feet (2.5 m)

### FOSSIL FINDS

What's New York famous for? Yeah, a city full of skyscrapers, Broadway theaters and Fifth Avenue shops. But New York state has one other big claim to fame: hundreds of eurypterid finds, including the first one ever, in 1818. In fact, the sea scorpion is the designated state fossil.

# TENTACLED TERROR

## CAMEROCERAS

Modern nautiloids swim in the seas around Australia and the Philippines. They live in shells, look pretty, and are only about 8 inches (20 centimeters) long. They certainly can't do any harm to a sizable creature. Well, check out this nautiloid—it's called *Cameroceras*. It's longer than an average minivan, and it's a ruthless predator—as this crocodile would surely admit.

*Cameroceras* is using its tangle of grasping tentacles to drag its prey toward its beak. And you wouldn't want to go anywhere near that beak. It could crunch straight through hard shells—so the armored scales of this small crocodile aren't going to give it too much trouble. And worse is to come. Modern nautiloids have a toothed tongue known as a radula. This allows them to scrape and cut out the soft, fleshy parts of its victim. Scientists think *Cameroceras* would have had exactly the same tongue. Imagine if *Cameroceras* lived alongside modern sea creatures. It's hard to pity a vicious creature like a crocodile, but in this case, perhaps it deserves a little sympathy.

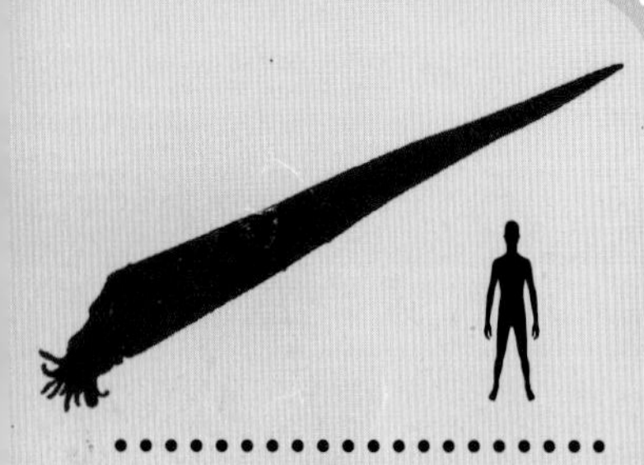

**CAMEROCERAS**

**PRONOUNCED**

Cam-eh-RO-seh-rass

**LIVED**

Northern seas,
470 million–451 million years ago

**LENGTH**

Up to 20 feet (6 m)

## HEAVILY ARMED

Modern nautiloids have up to ninety-four tentacles. Why do they need so many? Some tentacles are used to touch and sense chemicals. Some bring food to its beak. These ones are coated with a sticky substance to help the food stay on!

# PART BEAST, PART BATTLESHIP

## DUNKLEOSTEUS

This dolphin might look as if it is getting away from the huge, superpowerful fish, *Dunkleosteus*. But *Dunkleosteus* does not actually have to catch the dolphin. All it needs to do is get close and open its mouth. It can do this in one-fiftieth of a second—so quickly that it would create a suction force to pull the dolphin back into its mouth. And once it has its prey in its jaws, there is no hope. *Dunkleosteus*' bite force has been estimated at 1,100 pounds (5,000 Newtons)—that's more powerful than the bite of a lion, tiger, or hyena!

Not surprisingly, *Dunkleosteus* was an apex predator in its time—this means that no other creature preyed upon it. However, *Dunkleosteus* did have to watch out for one other animal—fellow *Dunkleosteus*. Some fossils show injuries created by the razor-sharp plating of other *Dunkleosteus*. Maybe they fought over territory—or, more likely, they were simply trying to eat each other.

**DUNKLEOSTEUS**

**PRONOUNCED**
Dun-kul-OSS-tee-us

**LIVED**
Shallow seas worldwide, 380 million–360 million years ago

**LENGTH**
Up to 33 feet (10 m)

**WEIGHT**
3.3–4.4 tons (3–4 metric tons)

## ARMOR-PLATED

*Dunkleosteus* was one of a group of armored fish known as placoderms, which means "plate-skinned" in Greek. Its skull was about 4 feet (1.3 m) wide and had armor-plating all around it. The plating was up to 2 inches (5 cm) thick, but at the jaws, this thinned down to razor-sharp edges. These made perfect blades for crushing fish.

# STRETCH-NECKED SAVAGE

## TANYSTROPHEUS

Who needs a fishing rod when you have a neck 10 feet (3 m) long? This is *Tanystropheus*, and modern scientists believe its super-stretched neck helped it to catch fish. However when Italian paleontologist Francesco Bassani first discovered *Tanystropheus* fossils in 1886, he couldn't believe any animal could have such a long neck. So he decided he must have found the wing bones of a giant pterosaur—the flying reptiles that lived during the days of the dinosaurs.

Although we now know *Tanystropheus* definitely didn't fly, we are still not sure whether it lived in the water or the land. Scientists think it probably lived somewhere in between—near the shoreline. Its front legs were shorter than the back ones, which would have been perfect for leaning forward at the water's edge for feeding. It probably liked to feed at tidal pools, which would be restocked with new fish every time the tide came in. But it might have taken a dip in the sea if it saw some particularly juicy prey. Good thing *Tanystropheus* isn't around today to catch dogs going for a swim!

**TANYSTROPHEUS**

**PRONOUNCED**
Tan-ee-STROH-fee-us

**LIVED**
Shores of Europe,
215 million years ago

**LENGTH**
About 20 feet (6 m)

**WEIGHT**
300 pounds
(140 kilograms)

## TALL TAIL

*Tanystropheus*' neck was about 10 feet (3 m) long, half its total length. Its tail was almost 6 feet, 6 inches (2 m) long, a third of its length. But its body was only about 3 feet, 3 inches (1 m) long, just one-sixth of its length.

# LET'S GET FUNKEI

## PLIOSAURUS FUNKEI

Check out this monster erupting out of the sea with a humpback whale in its jaws. This big bruiser of a reptile is *Pliosaurus funkei*. It lived at the time of the dinosaurs, and you could call it the *Tyrannosaurus rex* of the seas. It measured up to 43 feet (13 m)—about the same length as an average bus. Its skull alone was bigger than a human, and it contained teeth as long as carving knives.

Scientists think that most of the time *Pliosaurus funkei* cruised around just using its two front flippers. But for a torpedo-like assault like this one, it also used its back flippers to gain extra speed and propel itself toward its giant prey. Of course, these days humpback whales have nothing to fear from any such random attacks—luckily for them!

### BIG PREY HUNTERS

Pliosaurs, with their massive jaws and teeth around 12 inches (30 cm) long, evolved to capture large prey including other pliosaurs, plesiosaurs (*see next page*) and possibly giant fish such as *Leedsichthys* (*see page 22*).

### PLIOSAURUS FUNKEI

**PRONOUNCED**
Plio-SORE-us-FUNK-eye

**LIVED**
Arctic Ocean, 150 million years ago

**LENGTH**
33–43 feet (10–13 m); skull: 6 feet, 6 inches–8 feet (2–2.5 m)

**WEIGHT**
24.5 tons (22.3 metric tons)

### 3D PUZZLE

Scientists only discovered *Pliosaurus funkei* in 2006. That's when a huge pliosaur skeleton was found on the Arctic islands of Svalbard, Norway. At first, scientists couldn't tell what it was and called it "Predator X." There were around 20,000 fossil pieces, and putting it together was like doing a gigantic 3D puzzle. Eventually, in 2012, they announced they had found the biggest pliosaur of all time, naming it *Pliosaurus funkei*.

# STICKING ITS NECK OUT

## ELASMOSAURUS

This magnificent beast is really going the extra mile, isn't it? It's an *Elasmosaurus*, a member of the plesiosaur family of marine reptiles that lived from 200 million to around 66 million years ago. It has been described as "a snake threaded through the shell of a turtle," but it certainly didn't have a shell. Its neck alone was about 23 feet (7 m), half the length of its entire body.

Scientists think it spent most of its time in the depths, so its heavy neck was buoyed up by the water. To eat, *Elasmosaurus* would swim up to a shoal of fish, probably from below to remain hidden, and then dart its head into the shoal to snatch fish. Its teeth were sharp and overlapped so that fish could not wriggle free. Then the prey would be swallowed whole, and begin the long journey down *Elasmosaurus*'s neck.

The surfer here is probably not in too much danger, though. *Elasmosaurus* teeth weren't designed for ripping into large prey. It's probably just coming up for air—or to find out what this alien creature is doing floating around on a piece of wood.

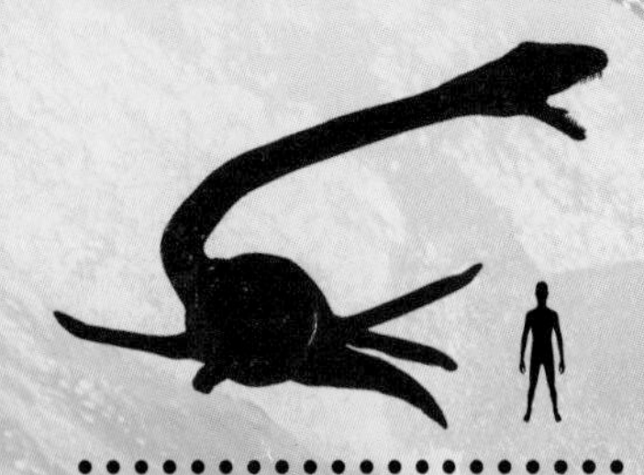

**ELASMOSAURUS**

**PRONOUNCED**
El-azz-mo-SORE-us

**LIVED**
North America,
80.5 million
years ago

**LENGTH**
Up to about
49 feet (15 m)

**WEIGHT**
2.2 tons (2 metric tons)

## A BIT OF A BONEHEAD

US scientist Edward Drinker Cope named the *Elasmosaurus* in 1868. Unfortunately, when he put the skeleton together, he placed the head on the tail! By getting the skull the wrong way around, the professor proved to be a bit of a bonehead himself. *Elasmosaurus* looks rather like *Tanystropheus* on page 14. But it lived about 125 million years later and was a much bigger and more terrifying creature.

# GIANT TOOTH

## MEGALODON

These days, killer whales are the undisputed rulers of the oceans. They don't fear anyone—even great white sharks get taken out by killer whales. It's not hard to see why. They can grow up to 33 feet (10 m) long and weigh a whopping 11 tons (10 metric tons). And their teeth can measure up to 4 inches (10 cm). This unfortunate sea lion is going to feel them . . . unless the killer whale feels *Megalodon*'s teeth first!

*Megalodon* was the biggest shark ever, about 40 times heavier than a great white. Its teeth were razor-sharp and serrated like steak knives. What's more, they were 7 inches (18 cm) long. Compare that with the great white's, which are only 1.2 inches (3 cm). Not surprising, then, that *Megalodon* means "giant tooth" in Greek.

### STONE TONGUES

Before people understood what fossils were, it was thought that *Megalodon* teeth were the tips of dragons' tongues. But in 1667, Nicholas Steno, the Duke of Florence's physician, realized that they came from an extinct shark.

### MEGALODON

**PRONOUNCED**
MEG-ah-low-don

**LIVED**
Oceans worldwide, 25 million–2.6 million years ago

**LENGTH**
About 52 feet (16 m)

**WEIGHT**
Up to 110 tons (100 metric tons)

### CAR CRUSHER!

It wasn't just the size of its teeth that made *Megalodon* so fearsome, it was the force with which it used them. In 2012, scientists estimated its bite was more than 3 times more powerful than that of *Tyrannosaurus rex* and almost 50 times more than a lion's—enough to crush a small car, or a killer whale.

# BIG MOUTH

## LEEDSICHTHYS

This fish might look terrifying, and it did have 40,000 teeth, but it wasn't a predatory animal. Like today's blue whale, *Leedsichthys* lived on zooplankton: tiny animals, including shrimp, fish, and jellyfish, that float near the surface of the sea. To get as much zooplankton as possible, *Leedsichthys* opened its mouth wide and only used its teeth to filter out the zooplankton from the seawater. Still, these kids want to watch out—that mouth is over 6 feet, 6 inches (2 m) wide, and they don't want to end up with the zooplankton!

Unfortunately, lots about *Leedsichthys* remains mysterious, and scientists have continually changed their minds about how big it is. At the start of the twentieth century, they thought it was 30 feet (9 m) long. But by the end of the century, they estimated it was more than 100 feet (30 m). Now it has been downsized to 54 feet (16.5 m). It won't surprise you that the Latin name of this creature is *Leedsichthys problematicus*. It has proved very problematicus indeed! But one thing is for certain: it is the biggest bony fish ever discovered. (*Megalodon* was bigger, but sharks have skeletons made of cartilage, not bone, so they are not classified as bony fish.)

### LEEDSICHTHYS

**PRONOUNCED**
Leeds-ICK-thiss

**LIVED**
European and South American seas, 165 million–155 million years ago

**LENGTH**
Up to 54 feet (16.5 m)

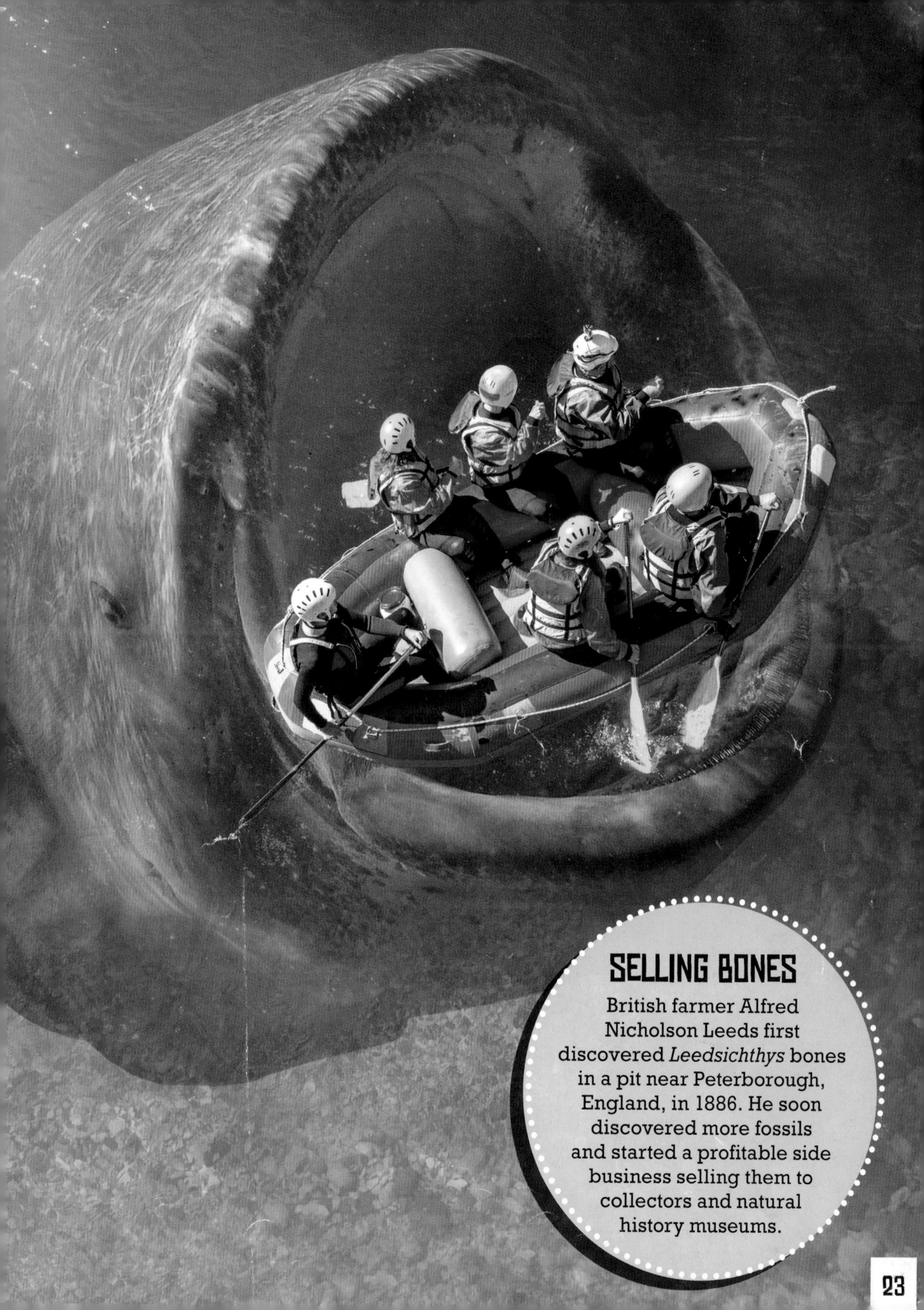

## SELLING BONES

British farmer Alfred Nicholson Leeds first discovered *Leedsichthys* bones in a pit near Peterborough, England, in 1886. He soon discovered more fossils and started a profitable side business selling them to collectors and natural history museums.

# A WHALE OF A TIME

## LIVYATAN

Wow, the fishermen on this boat have a front-row view of some amazing action! This ginormous creature is *Livyatan*, the biggest predatory whale ever known. It lived about 12 million years ago and probably ate almost anything that came its way—other whales, as well as dolphins, porpoises, sharks, sea turtles, seals, and seabirds, have been found at the site where the remains of *Livyatan* have been excavated. One thing is certain: it needed a lot food to keep its 50-foot (15 m) body going.

Scientists think it may have attacked from below, approaching from the murky depths and slamming into its target from underneath like a rocket fired from the sea floor. This has been called the Polaris attack, named after a submarine-launched missile. And it's worked here because it has successfully nabbed a hammerhead shark. Now the fishermen have to hope that it doesn't land back on their boat!

**LIVYATAN**

**PRONOUNCED**
Li-VIE-ah-tan

**LIVED**
Shores of South America, 13 million–12 million years ago

**LENGTH**
About 50 feet (15 m); skull: 10 feet (3 m) long

## HUGE TEETH

*Livyatan* is related to modern sperm whales, which roam the oceans looking for giant squid to eat. However, the sperm whale is a pussycat in comparison. It has small teeth and feeds by opening its jaws quickly so its prey is sucked into its mouth. *Livyatan*'s mouth was full of huge teeth, and, as you can see, it snatched its prey with a powerful bite, inflicting deep wounds, then tearing off flesh.

# SUPER SNAPPER

## XIPHACTINUS

*Xiphactinus* terrorized the seas at the end of the dinosaur era. Even though it wasn't the biggest marine animal, it was a great predator. So what did it have that other sea beasts didn't? First, with its powerful tail and wing-like fins, it was fast. With a top speed of about 37 miles per hour (60 kilometers per hour), *Xiphactinus* could swim towards prey—or away from predators—quicker than virtually anything else in the seas at the time. Second, it had vicious, needle-like teeth, 2.3 inches (6 cm) long and perfect for piercing scales and flesh.

However, it could not chew or slice off smaller pieces, so it ate fish whole.There are lots of fossils to prove this. Inside a 13-foot (4 m) fossil found in 1952 by Walter Sorensen in Kansas, there is a perfectly preserved 6-foot (1.8 m) *Gillicus* fish. Scientists think the *Gillicus*, in a desperate attempt to escape, ripped open the *Xiphactinus*'s stomach and damaged some of its vital organs.

So this *Xiphactinus* better watch out for the swordfish. Let's face it, it doesn't want that sword-like bill flailing around in its stomach.

**XIPHACTINUS**

**PRONOUNCED**
Zih-fak-TIE-nuss

**LIVED**
Seas around North America, Europe, and Australia, 100 million–66 million years ago

**LENGTH**
13–20 feet (4–6 m)

## UNDER WATER

Many *Xiphactinus* fossils have been found in Kansas. So how did lots of fish fossils end up in the middle of the United States? When *Xiphactinus* lived, the prehistoric Western Interior Seaway covered much of what is now North America.

## COMPLETE SKELETON

The Rocky Mountain Dinosaur Resource Center in Colorado is home to the biggest complete *Xiphactinus* skeleton. It measures 18 feet, 4 inches (5.6 m), and it took three experts three years to assemble.

# TIMELINE

## CAMEROCERAS

Named after the Greek for "chambered horn"

Nautiloids get their name from the Greek *nautilos*, for "sailor." The Greek philosopher and scientist Aristotle was one of the first people to study nautiloids.

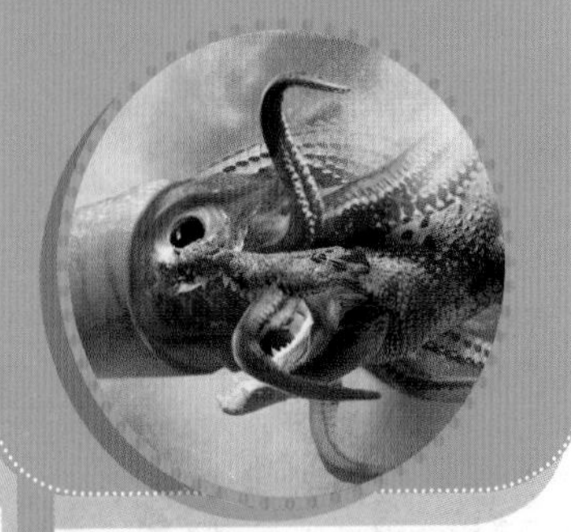

## EURYPTERIDS

Named after the Greek for "wide wing"

Sea scorpions or eurypterids lived for over 200 million years, longer than the dinosaurs. About 250 species are known.

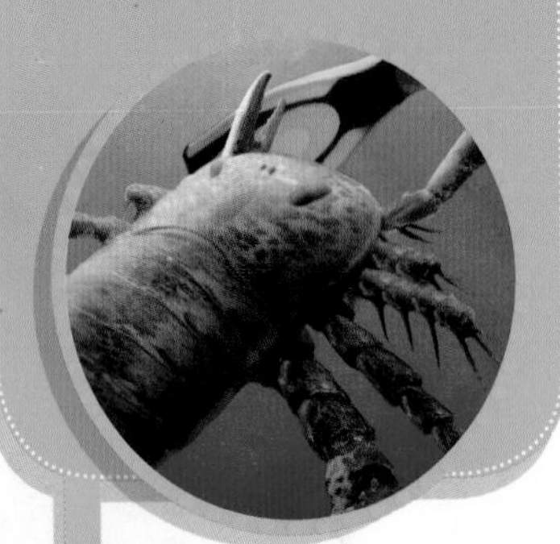

## DUNKLEOSTEUS

Named after its discoverer, David Dunkle, and *osteon,* the Greek for "bone"

Heavy *Dunkleosteus* was probably not a fast swimmer, so it probably went after slow prey or used ambush tactics.

## TANYSTROPHEUS

Named after the Greek for "long vertebra" (spinal bone)

A 16-foot (5 m) life-like robotic *Tanystropheus* was installed at Youth Park swimming pool in Taipei in 2013—and swimmers can actually ride it. Its creator, Masamichi Hayashi, has also made a robotic shark, whale, manatee, and sea turtle.

## LEEDSICHTHYS

Named after Alfred Leeds and *ichthys*, the Greek for "fish"

A tooth found in one *Leedsichthys* fossil proves that it was attacked, or at least scavenged after its death, by the vicious crocodile-like reptile *Metriorhynchus*.

470 MILLION YEARS AGO

Around 230 million years ago: First dinosaurs evolve

## ELASMOSAURUS

Named after the Greek for "ribbon lizard"

The group known as elasmosaurids ate stones as well as fish! Hundreds of them have been found in the stomachs of elasmosaurid fossils. Maybe the stones helped grind down the fish they ate, or perhaps they helped its balance.

## XIPHACTINUS

Named after the Latin and Greek for "sword ray"

*Xiphactinus* might have been a lethal predator, but it was also prey for larger fish. A fossil of the prehistoric shark *Cretoxyrhina* has the scattered bones of *Xiphactinus* inside it.

## MEGALODON

Named after the Greek for "giant tooth"

Scientists have had to estimate the size of *Megalodon* from its teeth and vertebrae. The rest of a shark's skeleton is made up of soft cartilage, which doesn't fossilize well.

## PLIOSAURUS FUNKEI

Named after the Greek for "more lizard" and Bjørn Funke, who discovered it

Pliosaurs were massive reptiles that swam the Jurassic seas. There are five other known species of *Pliosaurus*.

## LIVYATAN

Scientists originally called the creature Leviathan, after the biblical sea monster. But they didn't realize a type of mammoth was already called Leviathan. So it is now often named *Livyatan*—the original Hebrew spelling. The species *Livyatan melvillei* refers to Herman Melville, author of the whaling novel *Moby-Dick*.

66 million years ago:
End of the dinosaurs

2.6 MILLION YEARS AGO

# UNCOVERING THE PAST

Scientists who study the prehistory of living things are called paleontologists. To do their work, they study fossils, the remains of animals and plants preserved in rocks. Fossils of prehistoric sea creatures are often found on land because many ancient seas have shrunk or disappeared. Also, as the Earth's crust has moved over time, fossils that were once underwater end up on dry land.

***There are two types of fossil: body fossils and trace fossils.***

***Body fossils*** preserve the actual parts of an animal or plant. When an animal dies, it may fall into mud or sand and become covered by another layer of mud or sand. This enables bones, claws, teeth, and sometimes soft tissue and waste to be preserved. Mud or sand can also harden into rock and keep the shape and form of the body remains as a cast or mold.

***Trace fossils*** preserve the marks that an animal or plant has left. For example, an animal may have made a burrow, or a plant may have made holes where its roots once were. Animals also left tracks—these can tell us how fast it moved and give us clues as to how long its legs were!

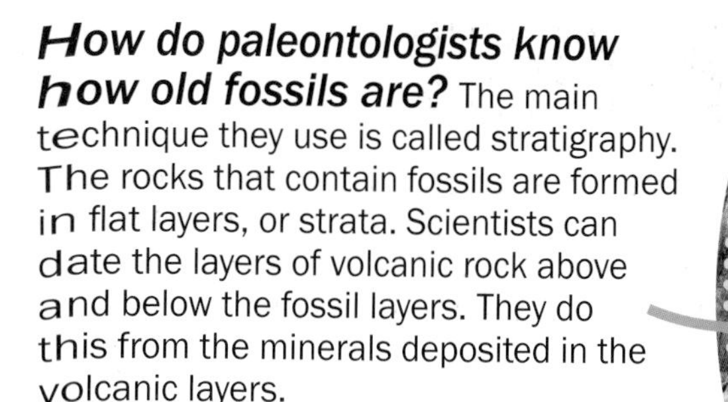

***How do paleontologists know how old fossils are?*** The main technique they use is called stratigraphy. The rocks that contain fossils are formed in flat layers, or strata. Scientists can date the layers of volcanic rock above and below the fossil layers. They do this from the minerals deposited in the volcanic layers.

So if a layer of volcanic rocks from below the fossil layer is dated at 230 million years, and a volcanic layer above is 240 million years, the age of the fossils must be somewhere between these dates.

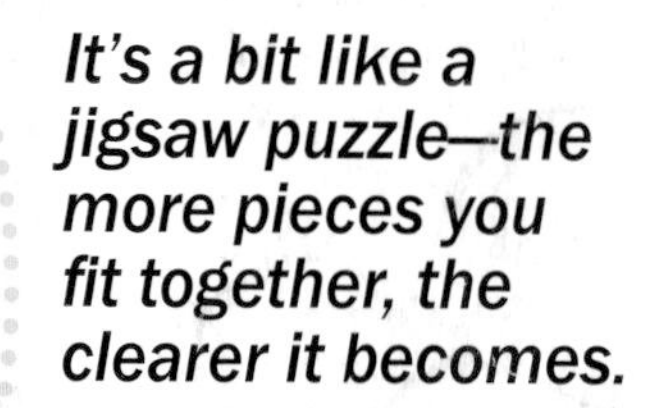

***It's a bit like a jigsaw puzzle—the more pieces you fit together, the clearer it becomes.***

You don't need to be a professional paleontologist to discover a dinosaur. You can join fossil-hunting groups instead. A seven-year-old boy from Chile found a new species of dinosaur. His name was Diego Suarez, and in 2015 his discovery was named *Chilesaurus diegosuarezi*. If you find a fossil of an unknown animal, it could be named after you!

# INDEX

## The Author

Matthew Rake lives in London, in the United Kingdom, and has worked in publishing for more than twenty years. He has written on a wide variety of topics for adults as well as children, including science, sports, and the arts.

## The Illustrator

Award-winning illustrator Simon Mendez combines his love of nature and drawing by working as an illustrator with a focus on scientific and natural subjects. He paints on a wide variety of themes but mainly concentrates on portraits and animal subjects. He lives in the United Kingdom.